# The Purple Caterpillar

Written by James Kelly
Illustrated by Veronica L. Williams

# DEDICATION

This book is dedicated to all the people of the world who are looked upon as being different, unacceptable, bullied, or set apart from what might be considered normal. Moreover, we want to acknowledge the everyday person who finds himself or herself prejudiced against because of race, creed, color, preference, or national origin. In addition, we want to remind people that the beauty in all of us comes from within—just open your heart and your mind and you will see it.

"Attention, class!"
said the butterfly teacher, Mrs. Kind,
to her class beneath a tree.
"The question was asked,
how will I grow up, and when I do,
what will I be?"

Her caterpillar students became very quiet
to hear what she had to say,
because they, too, wanted to grow up
to be as beautiful as she someday.

"You must eat your vegetables,"
Mrs. Kind, the butterfly teacher said,
"your grass, your fruit, and your leaves.
For this is the only way you can grow up
and fly high into the trees."

"Then, when the time is right,
you will make a cocoon
where you will live for many days.
And when you emerge,
you will be a beautiful butterfly
with wings to fly up and away."

(2)

"But what about Doogie?"
The tiny caterpillar named Margaret felt she
just had to ask.
Mrs. Kind, kindly questioned,
"My dear, I don't understand what do you mean?"
"Well, he is different from us," Margaret implied,
while the other tiny caterpillars laughed.
"He is purple, while we are all red,
or yellow, and some of us are even green."

"But listen, my dear," Mrs. Kind said,
"he is still the same as you and me.
He has six legs, and even twelve eyes,
to help him climb high into the trees."

"Yes, Mrs. Kind,"
The caterpillar named Jesse
decided to had to say,
"But he is purple, so he is different from us.
At least that is what my Dad told me, anyway."

Doogie bowed his head low,
and he tried not to cry,
as he wiped a small tear from his eye.
He did not feel different,
at least not until now,
so he decided to ask Mrs. Kind, "Why?"

(6)

"Why am I different?" Doogie quietly asked
as he slowly raised his head.
"Why am I not green,
or yellow, or even a shade red?
Why am I purple, and what does it mean?
Could it have been something I said?"

"No, little Doogie."
Mrs. Kind, the butterfly teacher,
tried to explain.
"We are all different in color, in shape,
and even in size;
no two of us are exactly the same."

"For instance little Marco
wants to be a moth,
and spend most of his day at play.
While Margo wants to teach others,
just like her classmate, little Mary Kay."

"Please do not laugh at little Doogie,
just because he looks different from all of the rest.
For I know, that when the time comes,
like all of you,
he will grow up to become his very best."

Having finished her lesson,
Mrs. Kind closed her book
and flew quietly up and away.
Then, as she disappeared out of their sight,
the tiny caterpillars began to laugh,
to sing and to play.

But they would not allow Doogie
to join in on their fun,
they did not want little Doogie to stay.
Doogie hung his head low,
and with a tear in his eye,
he began to walk quickly away.

(10)

All of a sudden, from out of nowhere,
the tiny caterpillar named Mary Kay shouted,
"Slow down little Doogie! Please wait for me.
Don't listen to what the others have to say."

"I know you look different.
But it's like Mrs. Kind, our butterfly teacher had to
say, we are all different, but what can we do?
Besides, I like it that way."

The tiny caterpillars, Doogie and Mary Kay, began
to get hungry as they strolled down the hill
toward a bush with leaves the greenest of green.
However, they noticed a very big problem,
as they approached the big bush,
a sidewalk was stuck in-between.

(13)

After talking it over,
a decision was made,
to carefully cross to the other side.
Even though, this sidewalk to them,
was so very long,
and oh, so very wide.

(14)

"Look!" shouted the little girl named Susie to a
little boy with a jar, not far behind.
"Here is a bug for my science project. Not
just one, but two, two different kind!"

"They are nothing but just dumb ole bugs," is all
the little boy named Willie had to say.
And as he tried to step on them,
the tiny caterpillars ducked down
and hid their tiny heads
as Susie, the little girl,
pushed the little boy Willie away.

(16)

"Stop being a bully," said Susie,
"And just listen to what I have to say.
We all need a chance to prove who we are
and down on the ground is the way."

"There are two caterpillars we could gather
and put inside your glass jar.
We could work on this science project together and
maybe both earn a gold star."

"I know you are smart, and I know you know how, so
ignore what the other kids have to say.
Let's team up together. Let's show them right now,
you have what it takes for an 'A'."

How could the little boy Willie refuse
such a simple request?
So Willie decided to do it by saying,
"That would be all right with me, I guess."

They scooped up the tiny caterpillars,
Doogie and Mary Kay,
and placed them inside Willie's glass jar,
and then carried them quickly away.

They took the tiny caterpillars,
Doogie and Mary Kay,
back to their second grade classroom
and put them both on display.

It was now Willie and Susie's responsibility
to feed these tiny bugs,
before class would begin every day.

The little boy Willie and the little girl Susie, would gather vegetables and leaves from a shrub, then store them next to the caterpillar's jar, on a table in the corner, inside a tub.

Finally, there came the day
when the tiny caterpillars, Doogie and Mary Kay,
would each make a tiny cocoon.
Their new home dangled from a twig,
that wasn't very big,
and really, took up very little room.

The children asked their teacher,
"Why did they hide?
After all, their jar is quite tall,
and really quite wide."

The children's teacher, Mrs. Gray,
tried to explain on that day,
why the tiny caterpillars, Doogie and Mary Kay,
had to hide away.

She explained that while inside their cocoon,
their tiny bodies would change
in a unique and strange sort of way.
Much like when little children grow up
or why a dog is no longer a pup,
we all change, day after day after day.

After hiding away in their cozy little homes
for what seemed to be nearly two weeks,
the tiny caterpillars, Doogie and Mary Kay,
appeared in a form that was rather unique.

Right before the kids' eyes
and to their surprise,
the tiny caterpillars, Doogie
and of course, Mary Kay,
did not look the same
as they did on the day
they made their cocoon
and decided to both hide away.

They were beautiful now,
as the children thought of how
the caterpillars had changed
from the way they first had appeared.

There was no fear
as the kids gathered near,
for these bugs were not strange,
nor creepy, or weird.

(26)

Doogie was the most beautiful of all.
He was brilliant shades of purple and blue,
and the most vibrant shades of green.
In fact, he was the most beautiful butterfly
these little children, and their teacher Mrs.
Gray had ever seen.

(27)

Mrs. Gray, the children's teacher,
was so delighted at their science project,
she hardly knew what to say.
She was so delighted, in fact,
that when she gave their science papers back,
she had given both Willie and Susie an "A".

(28)

While the butterflies, Doogie and Mary Kay,
were perched on a twig inside the jar
flapping their wings to dry,
the class had agreed
they should let them both go
so they could watch the new butterflies fly.

So the little boy Willie picked up his glass jar
and lead the children onto the school yard,
on this most beautiful and sunshiny day.
Once they found the right place,
Billy lifted the lid, and as soon as he did,
the butterflies flew out, and up, and away.

They flew out of the jar,
and past the schoolyard,
and landed on a bicycle
parked next to a car.

As they came to a rest,
short of making a guess,
they had to decide where to go.
Soon, Doogie and Mary Kay
were well on their way
as the wind began gently to blow.

(30)

They flew way, way up high,
as the kids waved good-by,
with the help from the nice gentle breeze.
And as they flew way up high into the sky,
they waved back, with a sigh,
then disappeared behind a large grove of trees.

The children were well out of sight
when Doogie and Mary Kay
looked down at the ground
at the place where they once used to play.

While they flew on their way,
they thought about all of the words,
that their butterfly teacher,
Mrs. Kind used to say,
of how you should make it a point
to be kind to one another,
each, and every day.

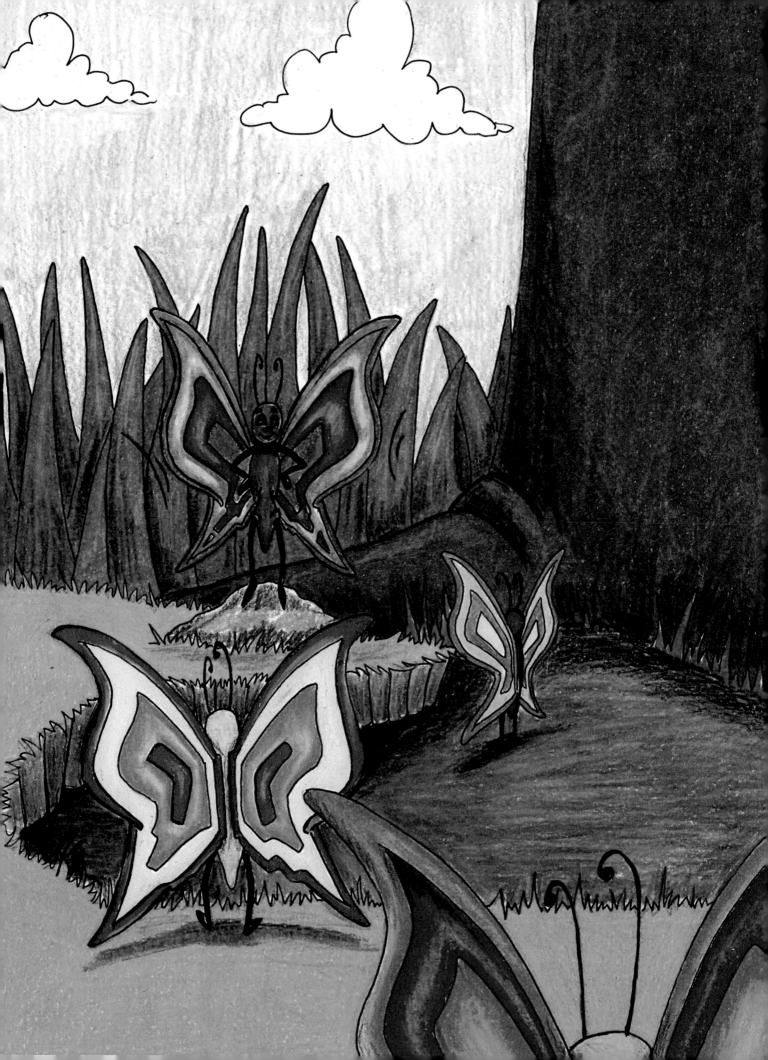

The two talked it over
and decided right away
to find Mrs. Kind, and thank her
for the wonderful things she would say.

As they flew near the ground,
their old caterpillar classmates gathered around,
now they were all beautiful butterflies, too.
But Doogie was the most beautiful of all
as he stood handsome, proud, and tall.
And in awe they had to ask,
"Doogie, is that really you?"

Mrs. Kind, their butterfly teacher,
could not help but overhear
what the other new butterflies had to say.
"Gather around," Mrs. Kind said loudly,
"It's time for one last class
before I send you all on your way."

The class settled in,
so the lesson could begin.
Mrs. Kind wasted no time
since she was running behind.

"You all laughed at Doogie,
except for you, Mary Kay,"
*Mrs. Kind said*, pointing her finger
as she turned her head.
"Take a look at him now,
and think about how
he is as beautiful as I once said."

"Remember the lesson
that I once taught you,
of the beauty that comes from within?
Of how you cannot see it,
but you can feel it.
It is time for that lesson again."

(36)

"You all think that Doogie, the butterfly,
turned out more beautiful by sight than the rest.
But the fact is that Doogie the purple caterpillar
grew up to become his very best."

"It isn't the colors that make him more
beautiful, or the way that he holds his head.
It is all the great things that Doogie does,
and all of the wonderful things that he says."

"When you do all of the things
you know that you should,
and do your best to treat everyone nice,
the beauty within
will begin to appear
without having to even think twice."

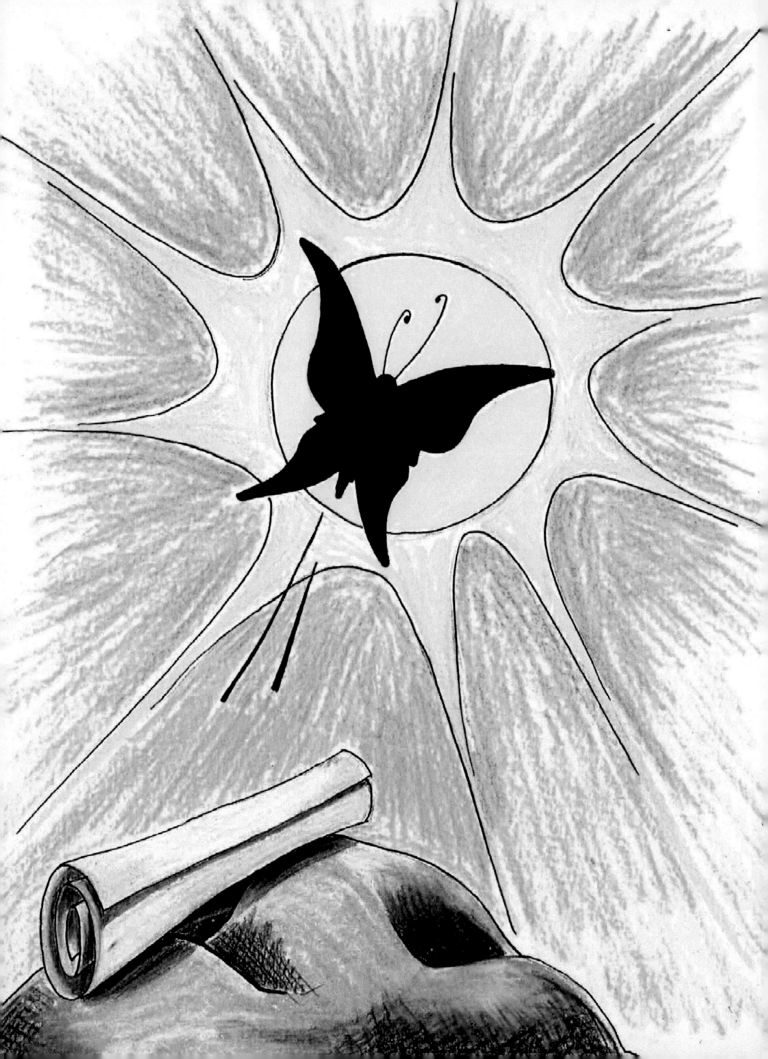

All the new butterflies
stopped for a moment to think,
having heard what Mrs. Kind had to say.
And after a moment, Mrs. Kind softly said,
"Class is dismissed."

Then, gently folded her book,
spread her beautiful wings,
and quietly flew up and away.

Made in the USA
San Bernardino, CA
19 June 2018